DRUGS

AND THE

MEDIA

SCARLETT MccGWIRE

Wayland

DRUGS AND CRIME
DRUGS AND THE MEDIA
DRUGS AND MEDICINE
DRUGS AND SPORT

Designer: Helen White
Series editor: Deborah Elliott

Cover: This disturbing image highlights the distance between imagery and reality that is sometimes fed to us by the media. Beneath the huge billboard advertisement for an expensive alcoholic drink sleeps a homeless, alcoholic down-and-out. Perhaps the effects of 'designer' drinks are not quite so glamorous as parts of the media would sometimes have us believe.

First published in 1992 by
Wayland (Publishers) Ltd.
61 Western Road, Hove, East Sussex BN3 1JD

British Library Cataloguing in Publication Data
MccGwire, Scarlett
Drugs and the Media – (Drugs Series)
I. Title II. Series 362.29

ISBN 0-7502-0328-5

Typeset by White Design
Printed by Canale C.S.p.A in Turin
Bound by AGM in France

CONTENTS

CHAPTER ONE

GOOD NEWS; BAD NEWS

IN THE 1970s the British underground newspaper *International Times* had a drugs column written by a woman called Maybelle. She gave a run down of the London illegal drugs scene – how much they cost and which were dangerous. It was rather in the style of wine columns in the quality newspapers of today.

A cover from one of the editions of the radical 1970s newspaper the *International Times*. The paper attacked conventional attitudes and views and gave a voice to youth disenchantment.

This is not the usual way the mass media treats illegal drugs. Drugs are not presented as possible best buys but shock horror probes on a menace that ruins people's lives.

The reason for this sensational approach can be understood by looking at the role of the media in society. As a whole the media both reflects and influences the values of society, and each publication or programme addresses itself to a particular audience. *International Times* was written by, and for, people opposed to many of the values of conventional British society. Taking drugs like cannabis or LSD was part of that rebellion, so the *International Times* was reflecting the values and needs of its young audience.

For the mass media, however, the target audience tends to be judged in terms of class, age or interest. Some newspapers are aimed at the working classes while others are written for the professional middle classes. Likewise, certain television programmes are specifically made for children or teen-agers. These differences do not affect the basic messages on drugs. Illegal drugs are dangerous. Prescription drugs can cure most illnesses and, hopefully, with time will cure everything: we are forever reading stories in the newspapers that the cures for cancer and AIDS are just round the corner.

The media is more ambivalent about alcohol and tobacco. It is accepted, by everybody except the cigarette

LEFT Alcohol is an addictive, yet legal drug. It can lead to illness and, in extreme cases, death. However, it is often presented, via media images, as an acceptable and important social activity. Advertisements feature glamorous people enjoying a drink, not hopeless drunks whose lives have fallen apart.

companies, that tobacco kills. However smoking is legal and many journalists and other opinion formers smoke. Young people are discouraged from starting smoking, but the banning of tobacco advertisements or the spread of no smoking areas are not greeted with universal approval but often written about as attacks on smokers. Alcohol is an even more complicated issue. Drinking is seen as a perfectly acceptable social activity,

RIGHT An example of the sort of sensationalist headlines that assail us daily in the tabloids, especially when drugs are concerned.

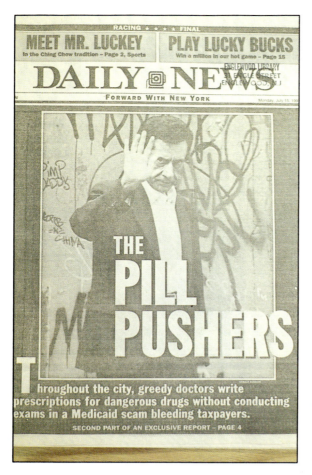

might be necessary to their jobs, but because they are entertaining and interesting. News does not reflect 'real life'. News puts certain aspects of a real story or situation under a microscope and enlarges them. Looking through British newspapers from the early 1990s, one might assume that most teenagers were illiterate, addicted to hard drugs and stole cars for nightly entertainment. Of course, in reality this is far from the truth.

News stories are unusual and they often contain drama or conflict. There is a saying among newspaper journalists that 'bad news is better news than good news': this means that stories about disasters and things that go wrong will always get into the papers before stories about life being wonderful. Illegal drugs are bad news stories: people are sent to jail, pop stars become addicted or the latest teenage drug fad is about to get completely out of hand. This list goes on.

Prescription drugs tend to make the news either when something goes wrong such as a hospital overdose, or when side effects are revealed to be dangerous. However, they can also be good news, such as a cure for anything from the common cold to cancer. New drug inventions are generally news stories.

with many articles and programmes praising champagne, whisky or even the humble pint of beer. Alcoholism is seen as something different and entirely unconnected to social drinking, an illness which happens to certain people, not something which happens to someone who 'just likes a drink'.

The media is a great deal more complex than a huge machine which puts out certain messages. All news, whether in print or broadcasting, is a mixture of information and entertainment. Serious newspapers contain a lot of information but are also well written. People read the articles not just because the information

CHAPTER TWO

CONTROVERSY MAKES NEWS

CONTROVERSIES are always good 'copy', which means makes a good story, because arguments are always interesting and because they allow journalists to put two sides of a question without revealing their own opinions.

In the drugs field controversy abounds. For over thirty years there have been arguments about cigarette advertising. Doctors and health educationalists have lobbied hard to get cigarette advertising and sponsorship banned while the tobacco companies, understandably, want to go on advertising. The answer has been a classic compromise of advertising accompanied by health warnings.

In 1991 the European Commission voted in favour of an advertising ban in the European Community (EC), which was voted against by Britain and Germany. The British media, in the main, did not report this as a health issue but an attack on freedom of the press because a lot of newspaper and magazine revenue comes from tobacco advertising. However, *The European* ran a story of a round up of views in the Community, headlined *'Stubbing out the habit'*. The standfirst, which is the large type which introduces a feature story, said: *'Tessa Thomas traces the history of the habit that is expected to be claiming around two million lives a year in Europe by 2025.'* The article concluded with reasonable scepticism: *'Cynics may question the EC's logic of suspending tobacco advertising – cutting manufacturers' profits and governments'*

tax revenues - while spending £2 million a day on subsidies for tobacco growers.'

A West Midlands newspaper, the *Dudley Evening Mail*, made no secret of its position as it ran a 'Campaign to Ban

Tobacco Ads' in 1991. Under the headline 'LIVES UP IN SMOKE. Each year 2,000 people in the Midlands die from smoking' an article begins: 'God knows what brand of cigarette brought death to a West Midlands home this week – but two children under nine and a widow grieve for the man who smoked himself to death.' Strong stuff!

Governments and health authorities have introduced anti-cigarette advertising campaigns to try and encourage people not to smoke. However, faced with the glamorous images and enormous budgets of cigarette companies, the campaigns are not having a major effect.

There is a debate behind the scenes about banning alcohol advertisements, but it has not gathered enough steam to get into the media. The main public debate on alcohol is over breath testing for car drivers. When breath testing was brought to Britain in 1970 there was an outcry. The media heaped venom on the Minister of Transport, Barbara Castle who was not only a woman but a non-driver. Public and media opinion changed dramatically over the next twenty years. Surveys now show that four out of five people want random breath testing introduced. At the moment the police must have reason to believe the motorist has been drinking before he or she can be breath tested, or there must have been an accident. Random breath testing means the police set up road blocks and test, say, every fifth car. The media is not convinced about this proposal. However, after a train hit the buffers at London's Cannon Street Station and the driver was suspected of having smoked cannabis, *Today* ran an editorial concluding: '*We welcome the coroner's recommendation that train drivers should be tested for drink and drugs after accidents. That is the least their passengers deserve.*'

Newspapers are forever seeking miracle cures to diseases. Huge sums of money have been and still are spent looking for a cure for AIDS and cancer. From the newspaper coverage one might imagine that drugs provide an answer to all our ills. A typical example comes from the *Today* newspaper in an article headlined '*Brain power pill*': '*A new wonder drug could bring fresh hope to people suffering from memory loss. The drug, Ondansetron, is said by its makers Glaxo to boost brain power. It is now undergoing trials in Britain but is not yet available to the*

The Daily Mail reported in November 1991 of a 'New Thalidomide Fear'. The headline and text concentrate on the Thalidomide tragedy of the early 1960s, rather than the real news - that the drug can treat some symptoms of AIDS and certain forms of leprosy.

New thalidomide fear

STUNNED VICTIMS FIND TRAGEDY DRUG STILL BEING USED

By JENNY HOPE, Medical Correspondent

VICTIMS of the thalidomide drug tragedy are fighting for new restrictions on its use.

They have been stunned to learn that dozens of patients are still being treated with thalidomide in Britain, 30 years after it was banned.

The controversial drug, prescribed to stop morning sickness in pregnant women, caused horrific deformities in their babies.

There were some 12,000 victims world-wide, including 400 in Britain, where a long and bitter battle was fought for compensation.

Since the drug was banned for pregnant women, doctors have discovered it can help a wide range of conditions. It has been used to stop life-threatening reactions to bone marrow transplants for acute leukaemia — which mainly affects children.

Thalidomide can treat some symptoms of terminal AIDS and help people with certain forms of leprosy.

Doctors also use it in curing Behcet's Syndrome, an immune system condition that causes devastating pain.

Agony

Women patients are warned they must not get pregnant. But Sheila Mottley, whose daughter Janette Cooke, 29, has all four limbs deformed, wants tighter safeguards.

She said: 'I want reassurances that the tragedy will never happen again. Many thalidomide victims don't realise

Bitter legacy: How the Daily Mail reported the compensation battle

public. In clinical trials in Italy last month 232 elderly forgetful people were given Ondansetron or a placebo (dummy pill) for twelve weeks. Those who took the drug showed improvements in their performance as if they were six years younger, says Glaxo.'

However, the side effects of these wonder drugs often cause disasters which are duly reported. Thalidomide was a classic case in point. Hailed in the 1950s and early 1960s as the solution to morning sickness in pregnancy, it caused deformity in many babies. The bitter battle for compensation was widely reported and *The Sunday Times* campaigned against the drug company. Thalidomide was no longer a wonder drug but evil. *The Daily Mail*

reported in November 1991 that Thalidomide can treat some symptoms of terminal AIDS and help people with certain forms of leprosy. However, this story was reported under the headline *'New Thalidomide fear'*. The report began: *'Victims of the Thalidomide drug tragedy are fighting for new restrictions on its use. They have been stunned to learn that dozens of patients are still being treated with Thalidomide in Britain thirty years after it was banned.'*

Even the normally serious *Independent on Sunday* newspaper whipped up the horror that the drug has come to represent rather than concentrating on what it is now being used for: *'Thalidomide, the drug which caused at least 12,000 children to*

This report appeared in *The Times* on 9 July, 1991. Attention is drawn to the word 'drugged', because drugs make news. However, the article is actually about elderly people being neglected in private nursing homes.

THE TIMES - 9 JUL 91

Old people in care homes are strapped to chairs and drugged

Harman: "Something is crying out to be done"

NEW safeguards to protect old people from abuse and neglect in private residential homes were demanded by Labour yesterday after a report detailed cases in which elderly people had been tied to chairs and drugged.

No Place Like Home, co-written by Harriet Harman, Labour's health spokesman, and published by Nalgo, the government officers' union, alleged that, in many private homes, defenceless people were being "abused, neglected, humiliated and degraded".

The report has dealt with cases decided by the Registered Homes Tribunal, the old people's homes watchdog, during the past two years, and the authors claim the cases are evidence of widespread maltreatment. Virginia Bottom-

The Labour party and Nalgo are demanding action after studying cases of neglect and humiliation in private old people's homes.
Philip Webster reports

ley, health minister, said yesterday that old people in private residential homes should be protected from abuse by more safeguards. She said, however, that to suggest that an epidemic of abuse was occurring was illogical and irresponsible.

Mrs Bottomley admitted there were problems and failings from time to time. "There are 11,000

registered care homes in England, but last year there were only 18 cases where owners of homes and registration authorities were in dispute," she said.

Cases outlined in the report include:
● a woman aged 90 who was tied to a chair and sedated;
● a home proprietor found by a tribunal to be unfit to have control. He had shown a total disregard for the law, did not appear for trial on some occasions and failed to pay fines. He had also shown a total disregard for and ignorance of the duties associated with running a home;
● residents being asked to live in attic rooms, which had to be reached via steep stairs, and to manage without central heating,

lavatories, bathrooms or wash basins;
● a home in north London where women were left in their nightclothes for the whole day, and were unattended for long periods;
● a home in Lancashire where residents had dirty bed clothing, and procedures for obtaining prescribed medicines for patients were unsatisfactory;
● a proprietor in London who administered drugs to a resident for whom the medication had not been prescribed.

The report also highlighted what it called inadequate staffing levels, and made 22 recommendations, which included barring owners who have run a bad home from starting another, laying down national guidelines for

staffing levels in homes and increasing the number of council inspectors of homes.

Ms Harman said: "The government rightly reacted promptly to recent revelations about wrongdoing in children's homes, but they are slow to act when there is evidence of neglect and abuse against old people ... If reading the cases in this report makes you fear growing old, then something is crying out to be done." The government was complacent.

Nalgo, whose members are responsible for inspecting and registering homes, called for more resources from the government, a proper staff training programme and better pay. John Findlay, its social services officer, said: "Although our report highlights some

very bad cases, our main concern is to ensure the best quality care in all residential homes. We want to ensure that the elderly, and all those in residential homes, are properly cared for."

He told a Westminster press conference: "Even though these are only a minority of cases ... one case of this sort is one too many."

Mrs Bottomley said: "There is no monopoly of virtue in the public or private sector, and things can go just as wrong in one as the other. We are determined to safeguard standards in all sectors." Reforms were under way to ensure regular inspections of registered homes, to help residents complain about abuse and to punish owners who broke the rules, she added.

be born with deformities in the 1960s is being manufactured again in Britain.'

There is a lot of controversy about the way prescription drugs are used in institutions. *The Guardian* ran a story in 1991: '*Social workers in Bedfordshire are boycotting a hospital psychiatric unit after claims by a teenage boy in their care that he was forcibly sedated by drug injections.*'

In July 1991 *The Times* ran a story headlined '*People in care homes are strapped to chairs and drugged*'. In fact the story was about a report saying that old people were not being given proper care in private homes for the elderly. There was one case of '*a woman aged ninety who was tied to a chair and sedated*'. The rest was more concerned with neglect, but the abuse of drugs was

highlighted because it is more controversial.

The media feeds on itself, so that, for instance, television programmes are reported in the press and often use stories that originally appeared in newspapers. Before Granada Television even screened '*The War On Drugs*' in 1987, the programme was making headlines. '*Anger at TV tips on how to sniff glue*'; '*Children to get TV drug use advice*'; and '*Row over TV drugs and glue shocker*' were just a selection.

A drugs worker was asked what he would say to twelve to thirteen year-olds about putting glue in plastic bags and putting them over their heads. Is that a dangerous thing to do? He replied: '*Sure, if they were doing that I would have no hesitation in telling them, if they are*

Glue sniffing is a worrying problem on a number of accounts. Products are cheap and, unfortunately, easy to obtain which makes the habit appealing to many young people.

determined to do it, not to use a large plastic bag, to use a small one.'

The questioner asked: *'Use a crisp packet or a small plastic bag?'* He replied: *'Yes, not to cover their nose and their mouth.'*

The questioner asked: *'You would show them how to sniff glue safely?'* The drugs worker replied: *'Less dangerously.'*

Granada wanted publicity for their programme. Controversy is news so they sent out a press release to the papers which began: *'Sniffing glue? Then don't use a big plastic bag to concentrate the fumes. Use a crisp packet. That is the advice a local authority official gives school children.'*

They certainly got coverage, but it meant the serious issues raised by the programme were not properly considered and the drugs worker ended up being severely criticized in the national press.

The biggest controversy about illegal drugs is legalization, although the debate is thought to be so subversive by most of the mass media it barely gets an airing. In December 1991 the *Daily Mirror* reported that a Women's Institute had voted to legalize drugs, and immediately quoted a local councillor explaining that these women did not understand the real world. In 1975 *The Guardian* ran an editorial about the legalization of cannabis which, in classic *Guardian* style, gave all the reasons for legalizing the drug, all the reasons for not doing so and came down firmly on the fence.

In early 1991 *The Guardian* reported on a European conference and summed up

A scene from one of the many legalize marijuana 'smoke-ins' that were held in Hyde Park, London in the 1960s.

the change: *'Twenty years ago discussions about the possibility of legalizing drugs tended to happen in the form of a 'smoke-in' at Hyde Park under the title of the 'Teddy Bears' Picnic' and were generally accompanied by arrests of long-haired participants.*

'Last week, the austere sociology department of the Free University of Brussels played host for four days to lawyers, police officers, doctors, drug workers, politicians and psychologists invited to discuss the theme of 'Prohibition or Anti-Prohibition of Drugs.'

The Economist found out what a minefield the debate was on 2 April, 1988 when it proposed *'a free market solution to the worldwide problem of drugs... (because) the attempt to prohibit the drugs trade is bound to fail, and in failing will cause worse evils than those it*

intended to cure...we want to see the trade legalized, controlled by government regulation, and subjected to government taxation.' The magazine was deluged with letters of shock and surprise and denounced by US Congresspeople – Republicans and Democrats. Mayor Ed Koch of New York City compared the magazine to those Englishmen who, in 1940, said the war against Hitler was unwinnable and advocated appeasement of evil.

A distinguished columnist of the *New York Times* denounced the arguments as capitulation in the face of evil. It was discussed by *Le Point* in Paris and *L'Espresso* in Rome. However, in Britain where *The Economist* is published it was ignored for almost a year and a half. It appears to be a controversy that the popular newspapers in Britain find too hot to handle.

The drug controversies the media is fascinated by often duck the serious issues or trivialize important debates. The controversies are concerned more with entertainment than information.

Ed Koch, mayor of New York in the 1980s, openly condemned the campaign to legalize drugs.

CHAPTER THREE

CRIME MAKES NEWS

DRUGS appear most often in the media when they are linked to crime. The media likes this because police swoops imply action. Television crews sometimes go out on drug raids, particularly in the USA and 'action footage' is screened showing drug squads in action. The media is very interested in the 'War On Drugs' and this coverage shows the 'good guys' winning.

In 1972 a survey showed that crime stories about drugs and the drug trade took up between eleven and nineteen columns a day in the *Boston Globe*, *Washington Post* and *New York Times*. That sort of coverage leads people to believe the drugs problem is far more prevalent and affects many more people than it does in reality.

It is not just the drug swoops which are reported but the ensuing court cases. These also demonstrate that the 'War On Drugs' is being won, but are also interesting because a conviction for drug dealing can result in a long jail sentence.

Often only the bare facts of a case are reported in Britain, although sometimes a particular case attracts wide media attention. Many of the cases involve people from India and Pakistan or Africa, but when white English people are concerned, particularly if they are middle class, the media becomes fascinated – an example of media bias and hypocrisy.

For example, when Simon Hayward, a British Guards Officer, was caught in Sweden with marijuana stashed in his car he protested his innocence and accused

A sensationalist headline illustrated with a provocative photograph, reports on the 'War on Drugs' being waged in the USA. The daily battle has given the media ample opportunity to report on drug swoops and court cases.

his brother of planting the drugs. The British press took up his case, criticized the fact that he was arrested, deplored him being found guilty and inspected his Swedish prison to see if the facilities were good enough. The Swedes pointed out, rightly, that the conditions were better than in any English jail.

Former British Guards Officer, Simon Hayward was arrested and found guilty of possessing marijuana, in Sweden. The British media reported the entire case with gusto, maintaining Hayward was innocent. The Briton was released halfway through his five-year prison sentence and promptly wrote a book about his experience. His high media profile ensured that sales were high.

Patricia Cahill and her father Patrick at a juvenile detention centre in Bangkok. Cahill and her friend Karyn Smith were caught in Thailand with 26 kg of heroin in their luggage. Members of the British press took up the case and tried to prove the women's innocence.

When two British teenagers, Patricia Cahill and Karyn Smith, were arrested in July 1990 in Thailand accused of carrying 26 kg of heroin the British press reported their every move. When Patricia Cahill was jailed for eighteen years, her father was reported as vowing he would get the people who 'set her up'. Just over a year after the arrest, *The Guardian* took up the case of Karyn Smith who had been jailed for twenty-five years. It ran a long feature in its Saturday magazine proclaiming her innocence and blaming Foreign Office bungling and police corruption for her long jail sentence.

In a story in December 1991 speculating on Smith's early release, *The Guardian's* crime reporter said: '*There has been bewilderment in official circles in Thailand about Britian's response to the jailing. Having been lectured by Western governments on the necessity to control drugs trafficking, the Thais have found themselves criticized over the jailing of two women found in possession of a vast quantity of heroin.*'

Another case taken up by *The Guardian* is that of the African women who act as drug couriers in a desperate bid to keep their families from poverty.

The media likes stories about the spread of the drug menace. In May 1991 the *Daily Star* did a special report: '*On the mean streets of Moss Side the kids on bikes aren't playing they are delivering hard drugs.*' The report explained: '*The*

Karyn Smith and her father photographed before her trial.

Daily Star has been out on the meanest streets in the land – Manchester's Moss Side, which has been dubbed the 'Bronx of Britain'. What we found was horrifying. Children as young as five are being lured into the drugs trade by evil dealers prepared to kill and mutilate for control of their patch.'

The article is a mixture of hype mixed with facts, a common practice of tabloid journalists. This could be seen when a feature in *Today* newspaper mixed a number of drug stories. The accompanying photograph was from the film *New Jack City* with the caption: '....*the violent new movie which has already led to one man's death in the USA after crack gangs saw it*

and went on a wild rampage.' The film had not yet been released in Britain. The headline read '*NEW CRACK CITY, UK: they could soon be shooting each other AT the movies as drug brings the Bronx to Britain.'*

The story jumped from a gang shooting in Manchester, apparently over crack, to a wounded police officer in North London to the showing of the film in New York, claiming it led to gangs running wild in the streets with one man killed and scores of other people injured. *Today* predicted that the same orgy of violence could be repeated on the streets of London, Birmingham and Manchester. When the film was released in September 1991 nothing whatsoever happened.

Another form of drugs' hype is the street value of drugs found on people when they are arrested. The rather inflated figures often come from the police because the higher the sum the more successful the arrest appears. *The Guardian* reported how the Court of Appeal ruled in 1991 that great care must be taken that the correct street value of drugs is put before the courts. In the particular case on appeal, two men had been convicted of importing £500,000 of heroin when it was worth less than £4,000. Estimating the street value of a drug should just be what it would sell for on the streets, but as drugs are often 'cut', ie mixed with another substance to make them go further, such as heroin being mixed with

The Sun report from 28 May, 1991, which told of the death of British UN official Don McIntosh in an air crash. The paper blames Thai drug barons, when in fact the crash was a result of a fault in the engine.

baby talc, figures are inflated. Sometimes they appear to be plucked out of the air.

Newspapers differ greatly on how they report drugs stories. A classic example is the relatively straight report in *The Guardian*. '*A young Texas woman was sentenced to twelve years in prison yesterday for possession of crack cocaine found in the body of an abandoned stillborn baby.*

'*Traci Jackson, aged twenty, was convicted last week of possessing the drug found in the body of the baby who was born prematurely after she visited a crack house.*'

This was converted by the *Sunday Sport* into: '*Evil junkie Traci Jackson, twenty-two, was jailed for possessing cocaine found in the body of her dead baby. She smoked the killer drug crack hours before giving birth prematurely, a court in Houston, Texas was told.*'

Another example follows the death of a British drug control agent employed by the United Nations (UN) in a plane crash in Thailand. *The Daily Star* announced: '*Human life comes cheap in Thailand.....The fact that 233 people died in the Austrian airline bomb outrage in order that a British UN official could be eliminated would not give Thai drug barons one twinge of conscience.*

'*Don McIntosh, the British agent working for the UN was their number one enemy. He was planning to set up a crime fighting network to smash their organizations.*' In fact the plane crashed because of a fault which led to one engine going into reverse thrust by mistake.

The Sunday Times argued that: '*Western narcotics agents in Thailand are doing more harm than good.*' The article says that: '*Mr McIntosh was not so much setting up a crime fighting network as* teaching the hill tribespeople to grow vegetable rather than opium poppies. Admirable though this programme sounds, it has created problems worse than it was meant to solve.'

Although a high moral tone is employed against drugs in all the crime coverage, the very coverage glamorizes them. They are tales of people jetting round the world earning fortunes, rather than the true picture of most dealers who use the drug themselves and sell it to pay for their habit. It is more exciting to deal with villains than pathetic people who are sad rather than bad. Patricia Cahill and Karyn Smith in their Thai jail might be a lesson to any teenagers tempted to act as couriers, but South East Asia can sound glamorous to teenagers stuck on bleak council estates.

LEFT Jack is twenty and lives in San Francisco, California. Jack deals in heroin in order to pay for his own drug habit which has left him jobless, friendless and homeless. He is in no way similar to the image of a drug dealer that the media often presents: a 'cool', glamorous individual with a chic apartment and an expensive sports car.

OPPOSITE TOP Canadian sprinter Ben Johnson. His disqualification from the 1988 Seoul Olympics for drug taking dominated the media for many months.

OPPOSITE BOTTOM A publicity poster for the 1960s Beatles record *Lucy in the Sky with Diamonds*, a reference to LSD.

CHAPTER FOUR

A POTENT MIX

gold medal winner Ben Johnson failed a drug test at the 1988 Olympics and had his medal taken away, it was headline news around the world. This was no unknown East European weightlifter, this was a man who had become a legend. One minute Johnson was the golden boy of sport, the next a cheat who had been stripped of his medals. Back home in Canada, where the press had gloried in his achievements, he stopped being referred to as Canadian but as Jamaican. The media, who had built Johnson up as a super star because he was a winner had begun to distance themselves.

ONE definition of news is that it is about people doing things and having things done to them. In most cases what the people are doing or what is being done to them is quite important. When those people are famous, almost anything they do is news. Most of us could walk down the street hand in hand with a member of the opposite sex and it would go unremarked. If Madonna did, it would be news.

Taking illegal drugs is news: it is unusual and against the law. When a celebrity does it, it becomes an excellent story. Athletes who take drugs to achieve better results always make news. When

Rock singer Janis Joplin was heavily involved in the drug culture of the 1960s. It was to prove her downfall, causing her death in 1970.

The media is part of the pressure on any sports star to win, for losers are ignored. Yet they expect perfect lives from the heroes they have built up.

One of the reasons given for the media's attack on sports stars who take drugs is the bad example they set as role models for young people. The most influential role models for the young are rock stars.

The more rock stars appeal to the rebellious side of teenagers and the more they appear to be breaking conventions, the more difficult their relationship with the media. They need to stay in the public eye to sell records, yet hate the invasion of their privacy as journalists search for scandals. Journalists themselves have the problem of not wanting to appear old fashioned but have to report any illicit goings on with shock and horror.

The link between rock and drugs has always been strong. In the 1960s, when the Beatles discovered hallucinogenic drugs, the group appeared to want to tell the world about it in songs like *Lucy in the Sky with Diamonds*, supposedly a reference to LSD. There were many groups who were more overt. While some sung about the wonders of drugs, others were dying from them. Janis Joplin and Jimi Hendrix were two of the best known.

Jim Morrison, who sang with the Doors, died in 1971. He was already a legend. His death ensured that his records were still selling in the same numbers twenty years later. The official cause of death was

American guitarist and singer Jimi Hendrix also died as a result of drug abuse in 1970.

Lead singer with the progressive rock group the Doors, Jim Morrison died in 1971. The official cause of death was a heart attack, but his drug and alcohol abuse provoked widespread media speculation.

Pop star Boy George was the media darling of the early 1980s, with his flamboyant and innovative image. His fall from grace was swift and hard as the media exploited stories of his heroin addiction.

a heart attack but there have been media theories ranging from a heroin overdose to murder. The stories glory in the large amounts of whisky and drugs Morrison consumed and the popular papers have tried to wreck his image. *The Mail on Sunday* said in 1991 that by the time he died: *'He was too fat to squeeze into his lizard skin trousers, and too shot through with drugs and whisky to stand up straight on stage.'*

Elvis Presley had begun his career by shocking US parents with his swivelling hips, but switched to being the epitome of the all-American boy, passionately against drugs. However, he only meant illegal drugs. By the time he died he was using prescription drugs to go to sleep at night,

to get up in the morning, as laxatives and to lose weight. After Elvis' death the media told it all.

Boy George was a singer with Culture Club, regularly topping the charts, when his heroin addiction was discovered by the popular press. Story after story vied for the most lurid tales: *The Sun* gave the 'Boy Junkie', as the paper dubbed him, only 'weeks to live'. As the *Today* newspaper put it: *'First he was the nation's favourite painted clown, then the classic fallen idol and object lesson in how to make a mess of your life.'* Boy George no longer makes the front pages, partly because he has fallen in popularity, but also because the story is now about the reformed junkie who has become a vegetarian, a Buddhist

The undisputed king of rock and roll, Elvis Presley. Drink and prescription drugs turned the once slim, handsome heart-throb into an overweight physical wreck. His death in 1977 still arouses media gossip and speculation.

and who no longer smokes cigarettes. One has to remember that 'bad news is always better news than good news'.

Steve Clark, the guitarist with the British heavy metal band Def Leppard died in 1991 after what the papers called a lethal cocktail of drugs and drink. *Today* newspaper told how he had been fighting a losing battle against drug and alcohol addiction, checking into several US clinics in the past few months. However, the headline read: *'Drugs kill Def Leppard rock idol Steve'*. This is technically correct because alcohol is a drug, but the implication is that his death was due to heroin or cocaine, because they are supposedly more 'glamorous' than alcohol.

It is not only rock stars whose encounters with drugs are reported in the media. Sometimes it seems as though every celebrity who has visited the Betty Ford Clinic in the USA for drug rehabilitation has been mentioned in the press. The popular press has constantly kept Britain in touch with Elizabeth Taylor and her attempts to 'go straight'.

The US edition of *Cosmopolitan* magazine ran an article in December 1991 about actresses who once were addicted to drugs. Many of the papers reprinted the facts. *The Daily Mail* reported: *'The Stars Confess.' 'Some of Hollywood's most glamorous female stars have admitted they were once hooked on drugs. Kirstie Alley, Whoopi Goldberg, Jamie Lee Curtis, Rosanna Arquette and Bette Midler say they have long since broken the drug habit. But Debra Winger admitted she enjoyed it – and has not promised never again to indulge.'*

The Betty Ford Clinic in the USA is famous for the number of celebrities who have gone there to 'dry out'.

A POTENT MIX

Movie queen Elizabeth Taylor's constant battle with drink and her numerous attempts to 'go straight' have provided excellent material for eager journalists.

In Britain the aristocracy is always news and the Marquis of Blanford's struggle against heroin addiction has been documented in the popular press. One profile of him in *The Mail on Sunday* said: '*He was a golden boy with everything to live for who transmuted* (turned) *his privileged existence into dross.*' Another article called him '*a self-pitying wastrel who became an intolerable burden to his loving family and adoring wife.*' He was dubbed a 'Champagne Charlie'.

For Mary Parkinson having a father, Cecil, who was a prominent Conservative MP, was enough to have her addiction to heroin revealed in the newspapers. Schoolgirl Emily Sheffield had two claims to her rather unfortunate fame when she was in the newspapers in 1991 following her expulsion from school for possessing cannabis. First the school was Marlborough College, a well-known British public school with fees of £9,400 a year as the papers gleefully reported. Secondly her stepfather was Viscount Astor which made her the nearest to being famous out of the three sixth form pupils who were expelled. Her expulsion gave the *Daily Mail* a chance to trawl through the history of the family going back to her step great

Star of *Desperately Seeking Susan*, Rosanna Arquette, admitted in the US edition of *Cosmopolitan* to having been addicted to drugs.

25

grandmother, Nancy Astor who was the first woman MP.

Drugs and celebrities are a potent mix, providing the sorts of stories that would have the news editor of any paper rubbing his or her hands with glee. Although assuming a high moral tone, the media associates drugs with glamorous, high spending people. A story about a celebrity who is against drug taking is never as important as a celebrity hooked on drugs, because 'bad news is better news than good news'. Although, of course, the best story is the celebrity who publicly condemns drugs and privately takes them.

OPPOSITE PAGE
Smoking a joint (cigarette made with tobacco and cannabis) at a rock festival in the 1960s. Cannabis, referred to by the media as 'pot', was very popular among young people at the time. It was the epitome of youth rebellion.

BELOW **James Dean – the original teen idol. His 'rebel without a cause' image of the 1950s has inspired generations of young people to adopt his mean and moody 'look' and to think smoking is cool. Dean made only three films (now classics) before his untimely death in 1955.**

CHAPTER FIVE

FACT OR FASHION

THE media documents all the latest crazes, particularly among teenagers who are seen as leaders of fashion, whether it is clothes, recreation, pop music or drugs.

In the late 1960s and early 1970s most of the media stories about drugs concerned cannabis, or 'pot' as the media, but hardly any of its users, called it. Newspapers were full of stories about hippy flower children and their exploits. Pot was more or less tolerated, although some stories certainly linked the new sexual freedom of that era with the drug. Similarly, in the 1950s it had been portrayed as turning virginal young women into sex-crazed beasts.

When the hallucinogenic drug lysergic acid diethylamide, or acid, or LSD became popular in the late 1960s the media withdrew its tolerance to illegal drugs. It revelled in stories of people taking LSD then killing themselves by jumping off tall buildings because they thought they could fly, or told of users going blind because in their 'stoned' state they looked at the sun for too long.

Tolerate or disapprove, the media gave the impression that most of the youth of that time were participating in the drugs craze. The question some people began to ask was how much was the media was encouraging it?

One academic puts the origins of glue sniffing in the USA down to two enterprising reporters from the *Denver Post* who wrote a story about the effects of inhaling glue vapour. The headline was *'Some Glues are Dangerous, Heavy Inhalation Can Cause Anaemia or Brain Damage'*. Denver at the time showed no evidence of widespread glue sniffing activity. However the scare headline, together with a detailed description with photographs of how to sniff glue to get high began a vogue for sniffing that spread through Denver and eventually the nation. Each local paper in turn used the same tactics, making the activity even more popular.

When glue sniffing was discovered by the British media, it was linked to the punk movement – fashionable in the 1970s and early 1980s. Glue deaths became material for lurid front page stories in both local and national newspapers. For instance, the story of a punk who leapt to his death made many of the national papers on 4 April, 1985.

Minor offences linked to glue sniffing became news: *'Glue Sniffers Used Bad Language – Fined £25 And Costs'* (local Scottish newspaper in 1984). Over the top responses by parents were portrayed as desperate attempts to combat the grip of glue: *'Glue Sniffer Locked in a Cage For a Year'* (*Daily Telegraph* 13 May, 1985). The media carried exaggerated warnings of the dangers: *'Death Games – As Deadly As Heroin, Yet As Easy to Buy as a Bar of Chocolate'* (*News of the World Magazine* July, 1984). Some of the descriptions must even have left some of the journalists

An example of some of the newspaper headlines that were common in the 1980s, when the media became aware of the dangers of glue sniffing.

Smoking crack, a crystalline form of cooked cocaine. The media had a field day during 'crack summer' in the USA in 1986. Newspapers, magazines and television screens were crammed full of lurid and shocking reports of the crack epidemic.

questioning the truth of what they had written, for instance: *'It takes a tanker load of glue a week to keep up with the demands of children in Wiltshire. That's how much they shift...gulping it into their lungs, wrecking their bodies, doing untold and in many cases permanent damage to their health and endangering their lives.'*

Panic was heightened by discovering ever younger glue sniffers: *'Mohican Aged Five. Head Says Boy Has Sniffed Glue. Robert Was a Skinhead at 3'* (*The Sun* 6 September, 1984).

Sniffing was linked to up and coming moral panics: *'Glue and Heroin Link Feared'*. *'The Bishop of Norwich...was given government backing in the Lords yesterday for his suggestion that research should be done on the link between glue sniffing and the availability of cheap heroin near ports.'* (*Eastern Daily Press* July, 1984).

At this time, heroin was battling in the media for the role of the deadly drug of the moment. In 1984 *The Guardian* noted that: *'Particularly among the young heroin has taken root as a lethal sub-culture which crosses all boundaries of geography or class.'*

The depressing documentation of young heroin addicts in Britain abruptly came to an end with what is known as 'crack summer' in the USA in 1986 when, as the *New York Times* put it two years later, *'The USA discovered crack and overdosed on oratory'*. Cocaine had been documented in Britain and the USA as the drug of the upwardly mobile, associated with the music business, films, advertising

According to the media, crack is rife in US schools. The media has, in fact, grossly exaggerated its usage – in 1987, 96% of high school seniors had never used the drug. Media attention and hype can often enhance a drug's appeal.

and the whizz kids of finance. Crack is a crystalline form of cooked cocaine which is smoked rather than snorted through the nose. It is cheaper and apparently far more dangerous than cocaine.

A National Institute on Drug Abuse (NIDA) survey on the teenage use of crack in the USA in 1986 and 1987 showed that 4 per cent of high school seniors reported having tried crack. This means that at the first peak of the crack crisis 96 per cent of US high school seniors had never tried it, much less gone on to abuse it or become addicts. In the midst of the crusade to save 'a whole generation' of our children from death by crack, the official data showed a national total of eight 'cocaine-related' deaths among people aged eighteen and under in the USA for the preceding year. There is no way of

knowing whether those deaths involved crack use or if cocaine was the direct cause of death: cocaine-related death means the dead person had tested positively for cocaine, but could for instance have been a passenger in a car in a fatal crash.

Two academics who studied the coverage of crack in 1986 described: '...an extraordinary anti-drugs frenzy. Newspapers, news magazines and television networks frequently carried lurid, exaggerated stories alleging that an epidemic or plague of drug use was attacking the USA.' In July 1986 three major television networks offered seventy-four evening news segments on drugs, half of these were about crack. Time and Newsweek each had five cover stories on the crisis during the year. Newsweek said it was the biggest story since Vietnam and

Watergate, the words 'plague', 'epidemic' and 'crisis' were used routinely. *Time* called crack 'the issue of the year'. A handful of national newspapers and magazines produced about 1000 stories discussing crack. Fifteen hours of television airtime on crack was carried by NBC alone.

In May of 1986 NBC nightly news said crack was 'flooding the USA' and had become the country's 'drug of choice'. Yet at the time there were neither any statistics showing how much crack was used, nor that it was the preferred way of using cocaine. When the first official data on crack was released a few months later it did not support the media view of crack. On the contrary NIDA suggested that 95 per cent of cocaine users preferred to sniff it rather than smoke it. In August the Drug Enforcement Administration (DEA) said: '*Crack is currently the subject of consider-able media attention...the result has been a distortion of the public perception of the extent of crack use as compared to other drugs...and that it presently appears to be a secondary rather than a primary problem in most areas.*'

The media and anti-drug public service announcements said cocaine was in-evitably addictive and crack users became almost instantaneously addicted. Yet according to NIDA surveys, two-thirds of Americans of all ages who have ever tried cocaine had not used it in the past thirty days. The number of cocaine and crack addicts was unknown in the NIDA evidence but the vast majority of more than 22 million Americans who had tried

The youth of the USA wage their own 'war on drugs'.

cocaine did not use it in crack form, did not escalate to daily use and did not end up addicted, in treatment, in hospitals or selling their mother's television set for a fix.

In order to claim that crack was 'the most addictive substance known' the media had to explain why. The reasons ranged from 'intense rush' through 'whole body orgasm' and 'better than sex' to 'cheaper than cocaine' – in fact a massive advertising campaign for the drug. The Americans who examined the media and 'crack summer' concluded that after months of being bombarded with such accounts the question is not why 4 per cent of US young people have tried crack, but rather why so many more of the other 96 per cent have not.

The British press jumped on the crack bandwagon in 1987, speculating on its arrival in Britain.

A Professor at the prestigious Cornell University wrote in 1987: '*I am concerned that this (unprecedented) attention (to cocaine and crack) is significantly contributing to the increased prevalence of cocaine use. Drug using behaviour is being popularized by a media that glamorizes and romanticizes it. Not only are these presentations ineffective as deterrents but they stimulate many people to pursue the drug experience.*'

A British doctor writing in the *British Medical Journal* said: '*So is crack the tiger or the toy poodle? In the light of the scientific evidence it would be wrong to portray crack as innocent fun. And yet to give crack the image of the mythological monster and portray it sensationally as something uniquely diabolical will only add to its allure.*'

The British press reported the US 'crack epidemic' with warnings of its imminent arrival, but apart from a few reports of crack on notorious council estates the drug never took off in the media. They had switched their attention to ecstasy.

Ecstasy is an artificially-made drug known in medical circles by the cumbersome name of methylene dioxymthamphetamibe. It was originally available in Britain as an expensive and decidedly upmarket designer drug but then spread to become the favourite among acid house party goers.

In the spring of 1988 the 'quality' newspapers announced its arrival in Britain with headlines like '*Yuppie ecstasy hits the street*', while the tabloids called it '*The Summer of Love*'. One of the tabloids ran a feature about '*groovy and cool*' acid house music with a 'guide to the lingo' and a special offer to its readers to buy an acid house T-shirt '*for only £5.50 man*'.

This _Daily Mail_ report tells of a _'Crack crisis in Britain'_. However, British media attention to the drug was short-lived. All interest was diverted to ecstasy, an artificially-made drug, which the press labelled 'Yuppie ecstasy'.

The realization that ecstasy was not a cosy, safe drug changed all that. The weekly magazine, _The New Statesman_ called it: '..._the most controversial stimulant to attach itself to music since the hallucinogenic days of the late 1960s._' The daily press went further with stories such as: '_Naive and adventure seeking youngsters were alerted to the summer's fun and flocked to West End clubs and underground warehouses where they were peddled LSD at vastly inflated prices._' One could ask if it was the newspaper stories which had first alerted these 'naive and adventure seeking youngsters'. When a young woman collapsed and died at an acid house party, even though the death was not drug related, the press looked for horror stories. Banner headlines announced: '_£12 trip to evil night of ecstasy_', '_Acid army of baseball bat brutes_', '_The Agony of Ecstasy_'. As in the 1960s, the papers found people attempting to fly and falling from roofs.

By the early 1990s ecstasy was old news. One newspaper announced that ice, which is smokeable speed, was likely to become the 'drug of the year (1992)'.

The question is how much the media coverage of the latest craze acts as advertising. Once ice was labelled the 'drug of the year', how many people set out to find it and try it?

OPPOSITE An ironic anti-cigarette advert.

BELOW The media linked ecstasy to the new youth culture of acid house. The symbols and icons associated with the new fashion revolved around the hallucinogenic effects of acid and ecstasy. There is no doubt that the intense and hysterical media coverage gave ecstasy a glamour and allure that attracted young people.

CHAPTER SIX

ADVERTISING AND CAMPAIGNS

IN 1985-6 the British government's advertising budget for campaigns to persuade people to stop smoking was almost £2 million. The cigarette companies spent about £100 million encouraging people to take up and continue smoking. Governments and the tobacco companies both use the media to get their messages across. Many governments even use advertising agencies for their campaigns. Does it work? This chapter looks at what happens when governments and the tobacco and drink companies pay for their messages to be in the media.

CIGARETTES

Over half the advertising budget in 1985-6 for anti-smoking campaigns in Britain was directed at teenagers. They are the group most at risk because few people start smoking as adults – only a small minority of smokers do not begin by the age of fifteen. In 1991 the illegal market of sales of cigarettes to the under-sixteens was estimated to be worth £90 million a year.

Cigarette companies deny that their advertising affects the under-sixteens. However, a lot of research contradicts this. Many children can identify cigarette advertisements which do not show brand names. Three studies have shown that under-age smokers tend to be more adept than non-smokers at recognizing and identifying cigarette brand imagery. In a study in Australia, under-age smokers were nearly twice as good as non-smokers at identifying cigarette advertisements and

brand slogans. This suggests they tend to be more aware of cigarette advertising.

Under-age smokers also tend to have more positive attitudes towards cigarette

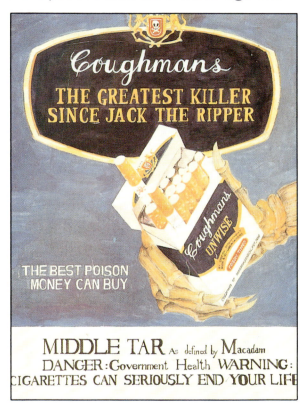

advertising. The researchers say that: 'These findings indicate that under-age smokers are getting some kind of pleasure, reward or reassurance out of cigarette advertising. In other words cigarette advertising is reinforcing under-age smoking.'

In a study of 6000 children aged between ten and twelve: 'Children who approved of cigarette advertising were

Members of the Australian non-smoking public decided to show their disapproval of a cigarette company's campaign.

twice as likely to become smokers as children who disapproved, with the smoking behaviour of those who were ambivalent about advertising falling between that of the two other groups... Children (who already smoked) who disapproved of cigarette advertising were more likely to quit than those who approved of it.'

In Britain cigarette advertising is banned on television and posters on billboards are not allowed in sight of schools. In the USA it is a free for all, with teenage movies in the forefront of the push. Huge sums are paid to get cigarette brands 'placed' in children's films. Philip Morris paid US $42,500 to have 'Marlboro' featured in *Superman II* in which (contrary to the comic book characterization) Lois Lane is a smoker. The company also paid $350,000 to have

another brand featured in the James Bond movie *Licensed to Kill*. In *Beverley Hills Cop*, Eddie Murphy holds up a pack of 'Lucky Strikes' and says: 'These cigarettes are very popular with the children.' In *Who Framed Roger Rabbit?*, detective Eddie Valiant is offered 'Lucky Strike' cigarettes by a teenage boy and 'Camel' cigarettes by the cartoon character Betty Boop.

Teenage girls are thought to be the most susceptible to cigarette advertising. The Cancer Research Campaign of Manchester University said: 'Advertising projects an image of smoking as a fashion accessory. Girls are more subjected to this image than boys because they tend to be more concerned about controlling their weight and about their appearance than boys. So they are more ready to believe that smoking helps them lose weight, or calm their nerves or look sophisticated.'

While young people may be susceptible to cigarette advertising they certainly appear to be most resistant to anti-smoking campaigns. The numbers of adult smokers have fallen rapidly in the past ten years, yet over a quarter of teenagers smoke regularly by the time they are sixteen, and this figure has remained constant throughout the decade. Perhaps the anti-smoking campaigns are doing something wrong.

ALCOHOL

Alcohol campaigns are aimed at stopping people from drinking and driving and encouraging 'sensible drinking'. The drink drive campaigns have been successful in not only bringing the numbers down but also, far more importantly, changing public attitudes. The campaigns to reduce drinking are harder to evaluate. Once again the campaigners are up against the industry, who spend vast sums of money encouraging people to choose their particular brand. Health campaigners argue that alcohol advertising is one element of a combination of pressures on people to drink. Alcohol advertising has very firm guidelines.

The restriction of times when alcohol advertisements can be shown, ie not between 4 o'clock and 6 o'clock on weekdays or around any childrens'

This advertisement for an alcoholic drink is in sharp contrast to the reality of life on the streets of Lagos.

programmes, is clearly only a limited protection. A survey carried out by the Association of Market Survey organizations showed that beer commercials were: '...*the second favourite advertisements for eleven and twelve year olds, third for nine and ten year olds and fourth favourite for six to eight year olds.*'

A MORI survey in 1990 showed a quarter of young men agreed that *some beer/lager ads make you want to buy that brand*', rising to 31 per cent of those drinking above sensible limits.

ILLEGAL DRUGS

Illegal drugs have no paid advertisements to encourage people to use them, only campaigns against them. However, the evidence of some campaigns shows they may be acting as advertisements. One drug expert came to the conclusion that: *'There are a depressing number of studies which show quite clearly that people who have had drug education end up using more drugs than people who have not.'*

In the 1960s and 1970s there were fierce debates that the horror propaganda about marijuana actually increased its use among young people.

In the USA, the decades of prevention campaigns have resulted in 'boomerang' effects. The anti-amphetamine programmes of the 1960s alerted a new generation to the perils and pleasures of the drug. Anti-cannabis, LSD and glue campaigns were all followed by an increase in use.

In Britain in 1985 a campaign against heroin was launched by the government costing almost £1million, against the advice of almost all the professionals working in the drug abuse field. In fact the Advisory Council on the Misuse of Drugs said in 1984 that: *'Caution should be exercised in the use of widespread publicity... partly because of the risk that ill-chosen educational methods attach disproportionate importance to drug misuse and arouse in some people an interest which they would not otherwise have felt. National campaigns aimed* specifically at reducing the incidence of drug misuse should not be attempted.'

One researcher said: *'It is reasonable to ask whether increasing anti-drug use propaganda is a response to an increasing drug problem, or whether an increasing drug problem is a response to increasing anti-drug-use propaganda.'* Writing about the publicity campaign against heroin he continued: *'While it cannot be fairly suggested that television messages act as 'drugs commercials' in any literal sense or on any large scale, the extent to which the material serves to legitimize certain values and/or practices is unknown.'*

The Glasgow Herald, with the drugs problem on its doorstep, said: *'Too often campaigns were mounted just to demonstrate to a rightly concerned populace that something was being done.'*

US citizens have taken matters into their own hands and erected billboards in many cities warning of the dangers of illegal drugs.

CHAPTER SEVEN

STEREOTYPES

Newspapers use stories of personal misfortune, such as homelessness, to evoke pathos and arouse the readers' sympathies. The bottom line is to encourage people to buy newspapers.

IN general the media deals with people rather than issues. Issues are explained by stories about the people involved. These people come to represent everybody involved in the issue and become stereotypes. So rather than discuss the problem of illegal drugs, the media prefers to focus on the people who take drugs.

In the case of an issue such as homelessness, by and large a newspaper is trying to arouse our sympathy, and in some cases our money. The homeless people on whom the newspaper focuses will normally have children and will have tragic bad luck stories, usually about matters which were out of their control

like losing their job or an illness that meant they could no longer pay the rent or the mortgage. They will not be stories of alcoholism, heavy debts through gambling or anything which could be deemed their fault.

Drug stories also deal in stereotypes and are aimed at portraying a certain image. Two studies in Canada and Britain in the late 1980s looked at the discrepancy between the image and reality in heroin and cocaine users.

COCAINE
In May 1989 a Canadian newspaper published a story under the headline *'Drug*

An example of media hype. On the one hand the report is condemning cocaine, yet it uses phrases such as 'Champagne drug', making it potentially glamorous and appealing.

Death 'Epidemic' in British Columbia'. It told how twenty-nine cocaine-related deaths had occurred between 1987 and 1988 in British Columbia. The inference in the story was that the people who died were well-integrated people who were only moderate cocaine users. The story identified cocaine as the cause of death saying: 'Cocaine killed at least eleven people in British Columbia in 1987 and at least eighteen in 1988.' These assumptions lead to phrases such as 'a cocaine epidemic is sweeping British Columbia' and 'the drug path of death cuts across social and economic lines from bikers to businessmen, labourers to lawyers.'

The facts did not bear out these assumptions. The coroner's file suggested few could be considered well integrated with everything to live for. Most were long

time heroin or cocaine addicts living on the fringes of society. Thirteen had criminal records; twelve had severe personal problems; ten were alcoholics; and twenty-three injected drugs.

There are substantial reasons to doubt that cocaine was a primary cause of all these people's deaths. Most were the outcome of general deterioration resulting from a prolonged unhealthy and socially deviant lifestyle in which cocaine was one element. There was no evidence of cocaine overdose in any of the deaths. Nine out of the twenty-nine were not attributed to cocaine by the coroner. Out of the other twenty, seven had other powerful drugs in their systems.

The data on the extent of cocaine use in British Columbia contradicted claims of an epidemic. The researcher said: 'It seems *unreasonable to attribute deaths of physically deteriorated, socially deviant polydrug (use more than one drug) users to the drug they happen to be taking when they expire.'*

HEROIN

An Oxford researcher looked at the common assumptions about heroin which appear in newspaper stories and compared them with the evidence.

● Try heroin once and you're hooked for life.

There are three sub myths to this line:
(a) It takes very few uses of the drug to become addicted. *The News of the World*

Smoking heroin. An infinite number of stories about the dangers of heroin (sometimes conflicting) are put before the public daily. It can be difficult to work out what is the real truth amidst all the hype and sensationalism.

interviewed someone after their second time of taking heroin. Phrases were used such as, *'knew what was happening'* and *'fight off the craving'*. The person said: *'Take it (heroin) once and you'll be mentally hungry for it. Take it twice and you'll be physically hungry for it too.'*
(b) There is no such individual as an occasional user.
(c) Once an addict, always an addict. *The Sunday People* advised parents: *'Act quickly. Once hooked, addicts have little chance of breaking the habit.'*

The facts show there are occasional users of heroin who do not become addicted. Studies have shown that most people can give up the drug. When soldiers returned from Vietnam in the 1970s, those who had become addicted were detoxified. When they were questioned three years later, only 12 per cent had become readdicted.

● Heroin addicts continue to use the drug only to avoid the horrors of withdrawal.

(a) The symptoms of withdrawal are horrific. *The News of the World* graphically reported one addict: *'I screamed, shouted, cried and pleaded with him (her boyfriend) to give me some. I would hobble around like a cripple and all the time I had this terrible craving for heroin. It was all I lived for. I would have killed him if he'd turned his back. I'd have done anything for a fix.'*

The Observer warned: *'Every bone in her (a particular addict) body will ache. She won't be able to lift her head off the pillow. She will feel violently sick and will steal again – or worse – for heroin.'*

Compare that to an ex-addict's account which appeared in *The Times*: *'Actually*

coming off heroin is physically no worse than very bad 'flu.'
(b) Once addicted the user is no longer seeking euphoria but only trying to alleviate the pain of impending withdrawal. An ex-addict told *The Observer*: *'Being addicted to heroin or any other drug is an awful, painful experience. Belief that a 'fix' leaves you in a state of euphoria is nonsense. It just staves off the pain of withdrawal. I have never met a happy junkie.'*

Scientific evidence shows that 42 per cent of hard addicts in a survey got high once a day.

• Use of heroin leads to physical and mental deterioration.

The newspaper articles studied were full of phrases like *'the misery of addiction'*, *'degradation'*, *'human wrecks'*, *'horrors of addiction'* and *'devastating effects'*. With little real information the press manages to signify complete physical, mental and moral breakdown of an addict as a result of heroin use.

Research shows that even chronic use of heroin does not result in major damaging physiological or psychological effects, although there are complications due to the use of needles and cut drugs.

• Heroin addicts have to turn to crime to support their habit.

The newspapers point to the cost of supporting a heroin habit, which they estimate between £25 and £100 a day and describe poor, unemployed young addicts. There are no examples of criminals but the conclusion drawn is that the drugs explosion has brought with it a wave of thefts and violence. Women are portrayed as selling their bodies for heroin.

The research shows that the most readily available source of income for drug addicts is the sale of drugs, ie heroin to other people. No relationship has been established between opiate or heroin use and crimes of violence. Most of the addicts found to be committing crimes to pay for drugs also committed crimes before they took heroin.

• Continued use of heroin inevitably leads to death.

The newspaper stories studied used phrases like *'food of death heroin'*, *'dirty death dealing trade'* and *'a deadly trade'*.

Statistics from the USA show the death rate among addicts is falling. In Britain in 1982, 712 people died of chronic alcoholism. This does not include people who died as a result of their drinking, for instance in road accidents or of alcohol-related diseases. There were ninety-one deaths which were drug related – which means they had traces of an illegal drug in their body when they died, although it did not necessarily kill them. There are no separate statistics for heroin.

• Most heroin related deaths are caused by overdose.

The Daily Mail stated that supplies were so plentiful that street prices dropped to £5 for a small sample bag of heroin and so pure that many customers have died from an accidental overdose.

A growing body of evidence shows that it is not the strength of the heroin which is to blame for many of the so-called overdoses, but the powders which heroin is 'cut' with. Most heroin bought in the street has had large amounts of sub-stances such as talc, quinine and strychnine mixed with it to make it go further so the dealer makes more money. Another factor is using more than one drug at a time, so they react against each other.

However, despite the media's lust for shock, horror headlines and its exaggerated and sensationalist approach, there is no doubt that illegal drugs, such as heroin are highly dangerous and should be avoided. There are also myths about why people get addicted to heroin.

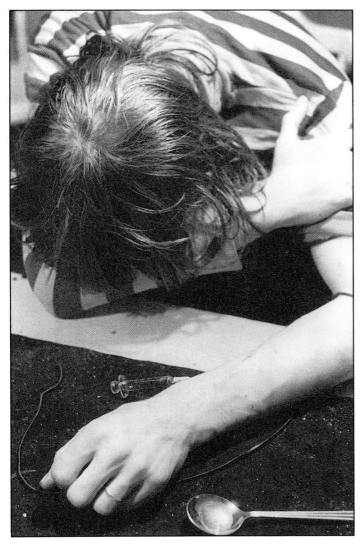

Crashed out after injecting heroin.

- **The proselytizing pusher.**

Articles refer to drug dealers as *'animals', 'merchants of death', 'dealers in death', 'racketeers', 'pushers'* and *'vile parasites'. The News of the World* announced that: *'Pedlars of death trap children in their evil web.'* It went on to say that: *'Schools have been plagued by pushers who try to tempt children to take heroin with free samples.'*

The research shows that most people who take heroin buy it from friends and most sellers are also users. In 1967 the US President's Commission on Law Enforcement and Administration reported: *'The popular image of the fiendish pedlar seducing the innocent child is wholly false.'*

- **The cause of addiction is the abnormality of the individual addict.**

The Guardian reported that the addict has limited resources for operating in our society, few educational qualifications and low self esteem.

In fact there is no answer to the question of what causes someone to be a heroin addict.

It appears from the two studies that in pushing drug stereotypes the media does not always stick to the facts. It might frighten people who never had any intention of trying heroin or cocaine in the first place. However, those people who know that stories are exaggerated might ignore the rather more important, and true, message: that these drugs are dangerous.

CHAPTER EIGHT

A BALANCED VIEW ?

MANY people in the USA during the 1980s believed that most high school students were addicted to drugs. The reason was simple: they had been reading stories about the menace of drugs in schools day after day in the press. When confronted with official statistics which showed a tiny percentage dabbled in drugs the public remained unconvinced.

The influence of weekly stories detailing the drugs influence was much more pervasive than one set of statistics: what advertisers call the drip, drip, drip effect.

The media is tremendously influential. A survey in 1990 showed that television and the media may represent the most important and unrecognized influence on adolescent behaviour in US society today. A study in Texas published in 1991 showed that television was the main source of information about drugs - parents and the printed media came second.

A 1985 study of drugs and television showed that alcohol is the drink most often seen on television – and the drug most often used on prime time television by actors, that is between six o'clock and nine o'clock in the evening. However, the problems associated with its use are largely ignored. Television news programmes remind us often of the perils of drinking and driving but a very different message is being broadcast on night time television entertainment.

The study showed that people who used illegal drugs were always in drug trouble, but people who used legal drugs

rarely had any problems. The reality is rather different: in 1984 a study showed that three-quarters of all substance abuse involves legal rather than illegal drugs. Prime time television does not reflect what drug use is really about in the USA.

The researchers concluded: *'Because today's children watch large amounts of television, such a carefree portrayal of potentially dangerous, albeit licit (legal) drugs may be helping to breed a new generation of problem drug users. Since alcohol and tobacco are shown being used by the 'good guys' with few negative consequences, an inexperienced audience may form attitudes that are conducive to using these substances frequently and in large quantities. With respect to illicit (illegal) drugs, the fact that these substances are shown as almost always producing negative consequences, frequently with dire results, may influence young people to disregard any messages about the dangers of these drugs presented by the media. Thus, the media may be exacerbating the problem of drug abuse by innacurately amplifying the problems associated with illicit drugs.'*

Not all academics who have studied the way drugs and the media interact would agree. Some would argue that even hyping the problem of illegal drugs at least brings it to everybody's attention. However there is a great worry throughout the West that the way the media approaches drug stories sheds light on the less important part of the problem, although it may be more 'glamorous'. A South African academic said: '*Although there is a small but growing problem of cocaine and opiate abuse in the country which should not be ignored, a more beneficial albeit less sensational aspect of substance abuse should be stressed by the media: the positive health and other effects to be achieved by the public if they were to use less alcohol and quit smoking.*'

Professor Griffith Edwards, head of addiction research at Britain's prestigious Institute of Psychiatry goes further saying that cultural myths about illegal drugs like heroin disguise the much greater damage being caused by alcohol and tobacco. He said that screaming headlines in lurid newspapers about drug-crazed criminals perpetuated the idea of addicts as alien, inherently weak, or fatally flawed in character, and totally distinct from normal, healthy people.

'*The pretence that addiction is only the needle and syringe, the deviant young, the blackmarket, and nothing to do with good citizens like ourselves is a myth that should carry a health warning.*

'*Tobacco in this country* (England) *kills every day on a scale equivalent to driving two crowded double decker buses over a cliff, and those deaths are generally unpleasant. Heroin and other injected drugs certainly constitute a major public health concern, especially so since the advent of AIDS. Meanwhile cigarettes kill between 100,000 and 150,000 people a year and more than a million people have an alcohol intake beyond the sensible limit.*'

The media does not give a balanced, informed view of drugs and many journalists would argue that is not their job. The media gives the impression that more people die from heroin than cigarettes. It gives misleading impressions because of the way drugs fit into definitions of news. Although it sets out to condemn drugs, in fact the coverage glamorizes them. All the evidence shows that anti-drug campaigns, be they for cigarettes or illegal drugs, also succeed in acting as advertising campaigns. Perhaps balance rather than hype might put the 'drugs problem' into perspective.

Our view of drugs is manipulated by the media. All the images, stereotypes and implications are there to make news and the more dramatic the news, the more people will buy papers and magazines. Issues such as the dangers of alcohol and cigarettes are not nearly so 'glamorous' as hard drugs.

GLOSSARY

Cannabis (also known as pot, hashish or marijuana) Literally, the dried tops of the flowers of the hemp plant. It has various dulling and euphoric effects.

Cocaine An addictive drug that comes from dried coca leaves. The drug, normally taken as a powder sniffed through the nose, produces a short-lived effect, dulls pain and makes the user energetic.

Crack houses Places where crack crews keep and sometimes manufacture supplies of the drug. The houses or apartments are heavily reinforced with metal doors. Crack is sold directly through a metal grate in the doors.

Detoxification Ridding someone of drugs and their effects.

Ecstasy An artificially-made drug with hallucinogenic effects.

Hallucinogenic drugs Drugs that cause the user to experience vivid and often bizarre hallucinations. These can be very dangerous in some cases, for example, when the user believes he or she can fly and jumps off a tall building.

Heroin A highly addictive and widely used drug which can be injected, sniffed or smoked.

Hype Enormous amount of publicity and coverage which makes something or someone extremely well known. Builds up expectations.

Legalization The debate as to whether or not certain drugs (cannabis, for example) should be made legal. Many people believe that by legalizing certain drugs it would remove the taboo, rebellious image and fewer people would try them.

Proselytizing Converting someone to believe in a way of thinking.

Subversive Trying to bring about change.

Susceptible Easily impressed or taken in by someone or something.

Tabloids Usually newspapers about 30 cm (12ins) by 40 cm (16 ins). They have an emphasis on photographs and often adopt a sensationalist approach.

FURTHER READING

Advertising by David Lusted (Wayland, 1988)

Alcohol Abuse by Brian R. Ward (Franklin Watts, 1987)

Cocaine Politics by Peter Dale Scott and Jonathan Marshall (University of California Press, 1991)

Drugs by Christian Wolmar (Wayland, 1990)

Learning the Media by Manual Alvarado, Robin Gutch and Tana Wollen (Macmillan, 1987)

Magazines by Kim Walden (Wayland, 1988)

Making Sense of the Media by John Hartley, Hooly Goulden and Tim O'Sullivan (Comedia, 1985)

Street Drugs by Andrew Tyler (New English Library, 1988)

The Drug Legalization Debate by James A. Inciardi (Sage, 1991)

The Politics of Heroin by Alfred W. McCoy (Lawrence Hill Books, 1991)

ACKNOWLEDGEMENTS

All-Action Pictures 25 (top); Associated Press/Topham 12 (both), 14, 15, 16, 19 (bottom), 20 (bottom), 23, 27; Mark Edwards/Still Pictures COVER, 37, 43; John Frost 4, 17, 28, 32; Jeff Greenberg 6, 13, 18, 30, 38, 45; David Hoffman 41; Impact Photos 39 (Penny Tweedie); Rex Features 19 (top), 20 (top, Ray Stevenson), 21, 22 (Brendan Beirne), 24 (Mathew Ford), 25 (bottom, Joffet/ Barthelemy Aslan), Wayland Picture Library 5 (both), 7, 8, 11, 35, 36, 40.

INDEX